Heinemann First
ENCYCLOPEDIA

Volume 1
Aar-Bar

Heinemann Library
Chicago, Illinois

© 1999, 2006 Heinemann Library
a division of Reed Elsevier Inc.
Chicago, Illinois

Customer Service   888–454–2279

Visit our website at www.heinemannlibrary.com

Series Editors: Rebecca and Stephen Vickers, Gianna Williams
Author Team: Rob Alcraft, Catherine Chambers, Sabrina Crewe, Jim Drake, Fred Martin, Angela Royston, Jane Shuter, Roger Thomas, Rebecca Vickers, Stephen Vickers

This revised and expanded edition produced for Heinemann Library by Discovery Books.
Photo research by Katherine Smith and Rachel Tisdale
Designed by Keith Williams, Michelle Lisseter, and Gecko
Illustrations by Stefan Chabluk and Mark Bergin

Originated by Ambassador Litho Limited
Printed in China by WKT Company Limited

10 09 08 07 06
10 9 8 7 6 5 4 3 2

Library of Congress Cataloging-in-Publication Data

Heinemann first encyclopedia.
        p.   cm.
     Summary: A fourteen-volume encyclopedia covering animals, plants, countries, transportation, science, ancient civilizations, US states, US presidents, and world history
        ISBN 1-4034-7108-8 (v. 1 : lib. bdg.)
        1. Children's encyclopedias and dictionaries.
     I. Heinemann Library (Firm)
     AG5.H45 2005
     031—dc22   2005006176

Acknowledgments
Cover: Cover photographs of a desert, an electric guitar, a speedboat, an iceberg, a man on a camel, cactus flowers, and the Colosseum at night reproduced with permission of Corbis. Cover photograph of the Taj Mahal reproduced with permission of Digital Stock. Cover photograph of an x-ray of a man reproduced with permission of Digital Vision. Cover photographs of a giraffe, the Leaning Tower of Pisa, the Statue of Liberty, a white owl, a cactus, a butterfly, a saxophone, an astronaut, cars at night, and a circuit board reproduced with permission of Getty Images/Photodisc. Cover photograph of Raglan Castle reproduced with permission of Peter Evans; BBC Natural History Unit/Rico & Ruiz, p. 40 top; Steve Benbow, p. 46; Getty Images/PhotoDisc, pp. 17, 42 bottom; Bridgeman Art Library, p. 33 top; J. Allan Cash Ltd., pp. 7 bottom, 13, 35, 41, 44 bottom, 47; Central Press/Getty Images, p. 32 top; John Cleare Mountain Camera, p. 10 bottom; Dee Conway, p. 43 top; Corbis, pp. 30 bottom, 42 top; Getty Images/Taxi/Al Michaud, p. 11; Hulton Archive/Getty Images p. 6; Hulton Getty, pp. 7 top, 48 top; The Hutchison Library/J.G. Fuller, pp. 8, 9, 14, 29, 37, 45; Oxford Scientific Films, p. 4; John Beatty, p. 36; G.I. Bernard, p. 21 top; Mary Chillmaid, p. 24 top; Clive Bromhall, p. 26; E.R. Degginger, p. 26 right; John Downer, p. 24 bottom; Michael Fogden, p. 23 top; C.W. Helliwell, p. 21 bottom; Manfred Kage, p. 39 bottom; Lon E. Lauber, p. 28; Andrew Lister, p. 22; J. Luke/PhotoLink p. 12; MPI/Getty Images, p. 25; Stan Osolinski, p. 15; Ryan/Beyer/Stone, p. 31; Alastair Shay, p. 40 bottom; Survival Anglia/Michael Pitts, p. 34; Survival Anglia/Alan Root, p. 23 bottom; Akira Uchiyama, p. 20 top; Babs & Bert Wells, p. 20 bottom; Belinda Wright, p. 5; Potton Homes, p. 27 bottom; Scenics of America/PhotoLink, p. 30 top; Science Photo Library/ John Mead, p. 10 top; Science Photo Library/A.B. Dowsett, p. 39 top; The Tate Gallery, p. 33 bottom; Werner Forman Archive, p. 27 top.

Every effort has been made to contact copyright holders of any material reproduced in this book. Any omissions will be rectified in subsequent printings if notice is given to the Publisher.

Welcome to
Heinemann First Encyclopedia

What is an encyclopedia?

An encyclopedia is an information book. It gives the most important facts about many different subjects. This encyclopedia has been written for children who are using an encyclopedia for the first time. It covers many of the subjects from school and others you may find interesting.

What is in this encyclopedia?

In this encyclopedia, each topic is called an *entry*. There is one page of information for every entry. The entries in this encyclopedia explain

- animals
- plants
- dinosaurs
- countries
- geography
- history
- world religions
- music
- art
- transportation
- science
- technology
- states
- famous Americans

How to use this encyclopedia

This encyclopedia has thirteen books called *volumes*. The first twelve volumes contain entries. The entries are all in alphabetical order. This means that Volume 1 starts with entries that begin with the letter A and Volume 12 ends with entries that begin with the letter Z. Volume 13 is the index volume. It also has other interesting information.

Here are two entries that show you what you can find on a page:

The "see also" line tells you where to find other related information.

This is the letter that the entry starts with.

Fact boxes give you details about the topic.

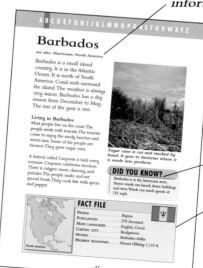

Did You Know? boxes have fun or interesting bits of information.

The Fact File tells you important facts and figures.

Aardvark

see also: Anteater, Mammal

The aardvark is a mammal. It eats insects. It lives in Africa. The word *aardvark* means "earth pig" in the Dutch language.

Aardvark families

Each aardvark lives alone. The female aardvark usually gives birth to one baby. The baby lives with its mother until it is six months old. The aardvark's home is called a burrow. The baby aardvark digs its own burrow. The aardvark sleeps in its burrow during the day.

INSECT AND PLANT EATER

Aardvarks use their long tongues to catch and eat insects. They also like fruit. They come out at night to eat.

AARDVARK FACTS

NUMBER OF KINDS	1
COLOR	brown to yellowish
LENGTH	4–6 ft.
HEIGHT	about 20 in.
WEIGHT	100–170 lbs.
STATUS	common
LIFE SPAN	10 years
ENEMIES	dogs, pythons, lions, leopards, warthogs

This aardvark is digging into a termite mound.

nose to sniff out ants and termites

long ears to help keep cool

nostrils close to keep out insects

20 teeth

an 18-inch-long, sticky tongue to catch termites

strong tail to hit attackers

strong claws to dig burrows and to find termites

an aardvark

Aborigines

see also: Australia, Australia and Oceania

Aborigines live in Australia. They were the first people to live there. They have lived in Australia for a very long time. Their stories and art are well-known.

Land and life

Aborigines live in family groups. These groups are called tribes. Some tribes live near the sea. They use spears and nets to catch fish. Some tribes live in the deserts. They are good at finding water and food.

Spirits and beliefs

Aborigines believe land is sacred. They believe that when they die, their spirits come back to the sacred places. They believe that the spirits of the dead can visit the living people. They believe in Dreamtime. Dreamtime is when the land was first made.

European people came to Australia 200 years ago. They took land from the Aborigines. They tried to make Aborigines forget the old ways.

Aborigines today

Aborigines live in all parts of Australia. A few still live in the old way. Today they are slowly getting back their land.

Aboriginal art often tells stories of spirits and the Dreamtime.

DID YOU KNOW?

Aborigines invented the boomerang for hunting. The boomerang is v-shaped. It returns to the person who throws it.

These Aborigine women are playing a string game with the children.

Adams, John

see also: Colonial America;
Jefferson, Thomas

John Adams was the second
president of the United States
of America. Adams was very
important during the American
Revolution. He signed the
Declaration of Independence.

Adams' childhood

When he was a child, Adams lived
in a farming community in the
colony of Massachusetts. He went to
school and church. Adams learned
to hunt when he was young. He
went swimming and skating.

John Adams became a lawyer when
he grew up. He married Abigail
Smith. They had five children. The
family lived in Boston.

Adams becomes president

After the revolution, Adams went to
other countries to represent the
United States. Adams was the nation's
first vice president. Then he was
elected president. The United States
was still a new nation. Adams helped
to make the nation strong. He was
the first president to live in the White
House. Adams later retired to Quincy
where he had been born. Adams
died on the fiftieth anniversary of
the Declaration of Independence.

FACT FILE

DATE OF BIRTH	October 30, 1735
BIRTHPLACE	Quincy, Massachusetts
DATE OF DEATH	July 4, 1826
PLACE DIED	Quincy, Massachusetts
PRESIDENTIAL NUMBER	2
DATES IN OFFICE	1797–1801
POLITICAL PARTY	Federalist
VICE PRESIDENT	Thomas Jefferson
FIRST LADY	Abigail Adams

DID YOU KNOW?

John Adams's son was a president, too.
John Quincy Adams was the sixth
president. He served from 1825 to 1829.

This is a portrait of John Adams.
He died when he was 91.

Afghanistan

see also: Asia

Afghanistan is a country in central Asia. The weather is dry. The winters are cold. The summers are hot. Most of the people live on flat land in the north. There are mountains and deserts in the south.

These Afghan women are winding wool from sheep or goats.

Living in Afghanistan

Many Afghans live in mountain villages. They raise sheep, yaks, and camels. They farm the land in the valleys. Their houses are built with mud bricks and have flat roofs. The houses are built on valley slopes.

Most Afghans wear long robes. Women often cover their faces with veils. People eat rice and drink tea.

Afghanistan had many years of war. This made life hard. Many Afghans had to leave their homes. Some people had to move to camps in the nearby country of Pakistan.

DID YOU KNOW?

The people like a drink made from yogurt. The drink is called *dagh*.

Asia

FACT FILE

PEOPLE	Afghans
POPULATION	about 28 million
MAIN LANGUAGES	Pushtu, Persian
CAPITAL CITY	Kabul
MONEY	Afghani
HIGHEST MOUNTAIN	Noshaq—24,612 feet
LONGEST RIVER	Helmand River—714 miles

Africa

see also: Continent, Desert

Africa is the second biggest continent. It is south of Europe. The Mediterranean Sea is to the north of Africa. The Atlantic Ocean is to the west. The Indian Ocean is to the east.

The land
There are plains in Africa. Plains are flat or gently sloping land. The highest mountain ranges are the Atlas Mountains, the Ethiopian Highlands, and the Drakensberg Mountains. The Sahara Desert is in northern Africa. The Kalahari Desert is in the south.

Climate, plants, and animals
There is a rain forest in the middle of Africa. The rain forest is hot and wet. Africa's grassland is called the savanna. Herds of animals live on the savanna. Some of these animals are wildebeests, zebras, antelopes, and elephants.

People in Africa
Many groups and tribes of people live in Africa. They live in 53 countries. Africa has towns and cities, but most people live in the country.

AFRICA FACTS

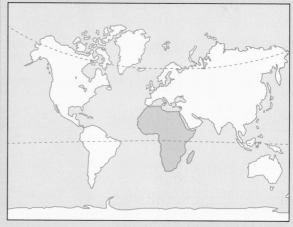

SIZE	about 12 million square miles
HIGHEST MOUNTAIN	Mount Kilimanjaro—19,340 feet
LONGEST RIVER	Nile River—4,145 miles
LARGEST LAKE	Lake Victoria—28,828 square miles
BIGGEST COUNTRY	Sudan

Cape Town in South Africa is one of Africa's large cities.

Air

see also: Oxygen, Pollution

Air is made of many gases. It is invisible. It has no smell. It surrounds the earth. Living things need air to breathe.

What makes air?

Air is made mostly of nitrogen. The rest of air is oxygen. When living things breathe in, their bodies use the oxygen. Living things breathe out another gas called carbon dioxide. When coal and wood burn they make carbon dioxide, too. Trees and plants take in and use the carbon dioxide. They then give out oxygen.

Dust, car exhaust fumes, and factory smoke can make air look hazy.

This climber has climbed very high in the mountains. There is less oxygen here. He needs an oxygen tank to help him breathe.

Dangers to the air

Clean air helps to keep people healthy. Smoke and exhaust from car engines make air dirty. Smoke and exhaust pollute the air. Dirty air is dangerous to breathe. Dirty air can hurt the lungs of people and make them ill. Cutting down trees is also bad for the air because trees make the oxygen that living things need to breathe.

Airplane

see also: Helicopter, Transportation, Wright Brothers

An airplane is a machine that flies in the air. It has wings and an engine. Airplanes and cars were invented at about the same time.

AIRPLANE FACTS

BIGGEST	Hughes H2 Hercules, wing span: 320 ft.
SMALLEST	Skybaby, wing span: 7 ft.
FASTEST	Lockheed SR-71 more than 2,000 mph

The first airplane

The Wright brothers built the first airplane that could fly. It flew at Kitty Hawk, North Carolina, in 1903. It only flew for twelve seconds. The first airplane was made of wood and cloth. Later airplanes were made from metal. They had powerful engines. Later airplanes flew faster and higher.

This is an early airplane flight by Wilbur and Orville Wright.

How we use airplanes

It used to take months or years to go far away. Now it only takes hours. Jumbo jets carry passengers and cargo all over the world. People use airplanes for travel. They can meet others in far away places.

This Boeing 747 jumbo jet carries more than 400 passengers.

Alabama

see also: United States of America

Alabama is a state in the southern United States of America. In the north, there are low mountains and hills. Most of the southern part of Alabama is coastal plains. Much of the state is covered in forest. Alabama has hot summers, mild winters, and lots of rain.

The State Capitol building is in Montgomery. It is similar to the Capitol building in Washington, D.C.

Life in Alabama

The land in Alabama is good for farming. Farmers produce cotton, peanuts, vegetables, cattle, hogs, and chickens. Manufacturing is the most important industry in Alabama. People make paper, clothing and textiles, chemicals, and metal products.

Birmingham is the largest city in Alabama. Montgomery is the second largest city. It was the birthplace of the African-American civil rights movement.

DID YOU KNOW?

The Confederate States of America was founded in Montgomery in 1861. The city became the first capital of the Confederacy. The Confederacy fought the United States in the Civil War until 1865.

The Montgomery bus boycott took place there in 1955–1956. Huntsville is the fourth largest city in the state. The U.S. Space and Rocket Center there is the largest space museum in the world.

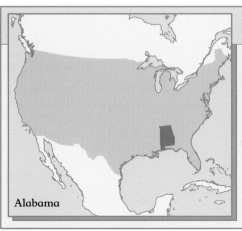

Alabama

FACT FILE

BECAME A STATE	1819 (22nd state)
LAND AREA	50,744 square miles (28th largest land area)
POPULATION	4,500,752 (23rd most populated state)
OTHER NAMES	Heart of Dixie, Camellia State, Yellowhammer State
CAPITAL CITY	Montgomery

Alaska

see also: United States of America

Alaska is the largest state in the United States. It is in the northwest of North America. It is separate from the other states. Alaska's Mount McKinley, also called Mount Denali, is the highest mountain in North America.

Life in Alaska

Alaska is rich in oil and gas. Producing oil and gas is the state's largest industry. Fishing is important, too. Alaska has many miles of coast to fish from.

The Alaskan wilderness

Some people in Alaska still hunt and fish the way their ancestors did. Many animals live in Alaska's wild places. The wilderness is home to bears, moose, wolves, and caribou.

The city of Anchorage sits between the Chugach Mountains and the coast of the Cook Inlet in southern Alaska.

DID YOU KNOW?

Alaska's flag was designed in 1927 by thirteen-year-old Benny Benson. The flag shows the North Star and the stars that form the Big Dipper.

Anchorage is the largest city in Alaska. The Iditarod starts in Anchorage. It is an exciting sled race that takes place every year. Teams of dogs pull the sleds more than 1,000 miles to Nome.

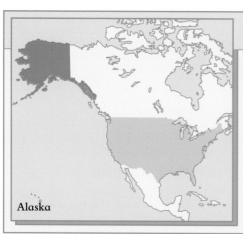

Alaska

FACT FILE

BECAME A STATE...	1959 (49th state)
LAND AREA.........	571,951 square miles (largest land area)
POPULATION	648,818 (47th largest population)
OTHER NAMES	The Last Frontier, Land of the Midnight Sun
CAPITAL CITY	Juneau

Albania

see also: Europe

Albania is a country in southeast Europe. Eastern Albania is cold. Trees grow on the mountains. Western Albania has hot and dry summers. The winters are warm and wet. The land is flat along the seacoast.

Living in Albania

Most people live in the country in stone houses. Houses in the town of Berati are built into the rock. The houses have carved wood windows and balconies. Many people like to eat cheese, yogurt, and meat. They also eat peppers, tomatoes, and carrots. Farmers grow grapes, olives, cotton, and tobacco.

The town of Schkodra holds a music festival. Some of the songs are from a long time ago when Greece ruled Albania.

This is Main Street in the city of Tirana. Modern buildings are built with balconies.

DID YOU KNOW?

Mother Teresa grew up in Albania. She was a well-known religious person. She helped poor and ill people.

Europe

FACT FILE

PEOPLE	Albanians
POPULATION	about 3 million
MAIN LANGUAGES	Albanian, Greek
CAPITAL CITY	Tirana
MONEY	Lek
HIGHEST MOUNTAIN	Mount Korab—9,029 feet
LONGEST RIVER	Drin River—94 miles

Algeria

see also: Africa, Desert

Algeria is a country in northwest Africa. It has seacoast, deserts, and mountains. Most of Algeria is in the Sahara Desert. The Sahara Desert is the largest desert in the world.

Living in Algeria

Most Algerians live near the coast. The houses are painted white. White reflects the hot sun to help keep the houses cool. People wear white clothing to reflect the sun's heat. A headdress keeps dust and sand out of their noses and mouths.

Algerians eat lamb. They also eat a flaky pastry called *brik*. *Brik* is filled with egg or meat and spices or olives. They also eat *tadjin*. It is a stewed, spiced meat cooked with fruit. They eat *tadjin* with couscous. Couscous is made from steamed wheat. Farmers raise sheep and grow grains, fruit, grapes, olives, and dates.

This is an open air market. People sit in the shade of the arches to keep cool. At night people sleep on rooftop terraces where it is cooler.

DID YOU KNOW?

Leather goods are made and used in Algeria. A goatskin pouch might even hold motor oil.

Africa

FACT FILE

PEOPLE	Algerians
POPULATION	about 32 million
MAIN LANGUAGES	Arabic, French, Berber
CAPITAL CITY	Algiers
MONEY	Algerian Dinar
HIGHEST MOUNTAIN	Mount Tahat—9,856 feet
LONGEST RIVER	Chelif River—450 miles

Alligator

see also: Crocodile, Reptile

The alligator is a big reptile. It lives in rivers, lakes, and swamps. One kind of alligator lives in the southeastern United States. The other kind lives in southeastern China. Alligators are relatives of crocodiles. An alligator's snout is less pointed than a crocodile's snout. Its teeth are different, too.

ALLIGATOR FACTS

NUMBER OF KINDS	2
COLOR	grayish-green or brown
LENGTH	up to 20 ft.
WEIGHT	up to 550 lbs.
STATUS	threatened
LIFE SPAN	up to 60 years
ENEMIES	Some birds eat alligator eggs and hatchlings. People kill alligators for their skins or to control the alligator population.

MEAT AND INSECT EATER

Alligators hunt during the day. They eat fish, frogs, snakes, turtles, and birds. Baby alligators eat insects and frogs.

an American alligator

eyes on top of the head for hiding underwater and seeing over the water

nostrils that close when underwater

strong tail for swimming

thick skin for protection

strong legs and sharp claws for walking, swimming, and digging

long teeth in a wide snout to hold food

Alligator families

The male is called a bull. The female is called a cow. The babies are called hatchlings. The female builds a nest made of mud and rotting leaves. She lays from 25 to 60 eggs. She covers the eggs with mud and stays close to the nest. She opens the nest when the hatchlings squeak. Then she carries them in her mouth to the water.

These hatchlings are keeping warm in the sun.

Alphabet

see also: Hieroglyphics, Language

An alphabet has letters or shapes. The letters or shapes stand for sounds. People use an alphabet to write all the words in a language. The word alphabet comes from the names of the first two letters in the Greek alphabet—alpha and beta.

Early alphabets

Very early people drew pictures to stand for words. Then an early alphabet was developed in Syria in 2000 B.C. Greeks and Romans made changes to this early alphabet. The English alphabet comes from the early Roman alphabet.

English	Greek	Arabic
A a	Α α - A	ا - · orA
B b	Β β - V	ب - B
C c	Γ γ - GorY	ت - T
D d	Δ δ - TH	ث - SorT
E e	Ε ε - E	ج - GorSH
F f	Ζ ς - Z	ح - H
G g	Η η - I	خ - K
H h	Θ θ - TH	د - D
I i	Ι ι - I	ذ - ZorD
J j	Κ κ - K	ر - R
K k	Λ λ - L	ز - Z
L l	Μ μ - M	س - S
M m	Ν ν - N	ش - SH
N n	Ξ ξ - X	ص - S
O o	Ο ο - O	ض - D
P p	Π π - P	ط - T
Q q	Ρ ρ - R	ظ - Z
R r	Σ σ ς - SorZ	ع - ·
S s	Τ τ - T	غ - HorR
T t	Υ υ - I	ف - F
U u	Φ φ - F	ق - Kor·
V v	Χ χ - H	ك - K
W w	Ψ ψ - PS	ل - L
X x	Ω ω - O	م - M
Y y		ن - N
Z z		ه ة - H
		و - W,OorU
		ي - Y,IorE

These are the English, Greek, and Arabic alphabets.

KEY DATES

4000 B.C. ..first alphabet

2000 B.C. ..first modern alphabet

1400 B.C...the Chinese develop an alphabet

700 B.C. ...the Greeks develop an alphabet

600 B.C. ....the Romans develop an alphabet

A.D.700 .....people use small letters and capital letters

A.D.800 .....Japanese develop a phonetic alphabet

A.D.1800 ..first Native American alphabet

The English alphabet

The English alphabet has 26 letters. There are two kinds of letters. There are vowels (a, e, i, o, u) and consonants. The letters of the alphabet are in a fixed order called alphabetical order. This order is used to list words in dictionaries and names in telephone books.

Not all alphabets look like the English alphabet. Some languages, such as Arabic, Chinese, and Hebrew, use other symbols for their alphabets.

American Flag

see also: Flag, Star-Spangled Banner

The American flag is the flag of the United States of America. It is a symbol that represents the nation. The American flag has other names. It is sometimes called the Star-Spangled Banner or the Stars and Stripes.

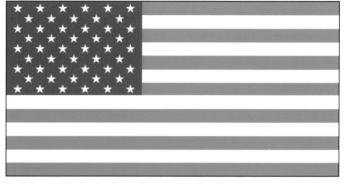

This is how the American flag looks today.

Stars and stripes

The American flag has thirteen stripes and 50 stars. When the nation was founded in 1776, there were only thirteen states. The stripes stand for those first thirteen states. Today, there are 50 states. The stars stand for those 50 states.

Flags everywhere

The American flag is used in many official ways. It flies outside government buildings. It is printed on stamps. Members of the armed forces wear a flag on their uniforms.

The flag is used in unofficial ways, too. Americans use it to decorate everything from clothes to cars to cakes.

Respect for the flag

Americans have customs that show respect for the flag. When it is raised or lowered, people should face the flag and put their right hand over their heart. The flag should not touch the ground. It should not fly at night unless a light is shining on it.

Public monuments and buildings often have the flag flying nearby.

DID YOU KNOW?

Congress approved a design for the first official American flag in 1777. The flag had thirteen stars and thirteen stripes. Over the years, the design changed. A star was added for each new state.

American Revolution

*see also: Colonial America;
Declaration of Independence;
Washington, George*

The American Revolution was a war. A revolution is when people fight to remove their government and form a new one.

The colonies
There were thirteen British colonies along the Atlantic coast of North America. The colonists could not make their own laws or choose their own leaders. The British government sent soldiers and forced colonists to pay unfair taxes.

The war begins
In 1775, the colonists began to fight the soldiers. The British army and navy often defeated the Americans. George Washington encouraged the Americans to keep going.

KEY DATES
1775 . . . . . The American Revolution begins.
1776 . . . . . The Declaration of Independence is signed.
1781 . . . . . Battle of Yorktown.
1783 . . . . . Treaty of Paris.

British soldiers surrender at Yorktown, October 19, 1781.

Independence
During the American Revolution, leaders from the colonies met together. In 1776, they voted to declare independence from Britain. They would unite the colonies as a new nation called the United States of America. On July 4, 1776, the Declaration of Independence was approved.

Victory
The war continued until the Americans won a battle in Yorktown, Virginia. A few years later, Britain and the United States signed the Treaty of Paris. The treaty said the United States was now a nation.

Washington led his army across the Delaware River on Christmas night, 1776.

Amphibian

see also: Frog, Metamorphosis, Toad

Amphibians are animals. They are found all over the world but not in very cold places. Young amphibians live in water. They breathe with gills. They develop lungs in the summer. Then they leave the water to live on land. This change is called metamorphosis. Adult amphibians breathe through their skin and with their lungs.

AMPHIBIAN FACTS

LIFE SPAN .. Most amphibians live from 5 to 15 years. Salamanders can live up to 50 years.

ENEMIES .... Herons, large fish, and snakes. People sometimes fill in the ponds where amphibians live.

5. A frog has long legs for jumping. It has webbed back feet for swimming.

1. Eggs (called spawn) are laid in jelly to protect them and to help them float.

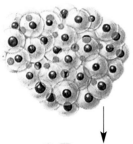

the metamorphosis of a frog

2. A tadpole grows in each egg.

3. A tadpole has a long tail to help it swim.

4. A tadpole with legs is called a froglet. Its tail will disappear.

Amphibian families

Amphibians lay many eggs in the spring. They lay their eggs in ponds and rivers. The eggs are called spawn. Baby amphibians are called tadpoles or larvae. Amphibians do not build a home. They live under stones or plants.

INSECT AND PLANT EATER

Small tadpoles and larvae eat water plants. When they are bigger, they eat water insects and other small animals. Adult amphibians usually eat worms, slugs, and insects.

Animal

see also: Invertebrate, Vertebrate

An animal is a living thing that can feed, move around, and produce young. Animals live everywhere in the world. They live on land, in water, and in the air. Animals are divided into groups. Some groups are mammals, birds, reptiles, fish, and insects. People who study animals are called zoologists.

LIFE STYLES

Nocturnal animals sleep during the day and hunt for food at night. Diurnal animals sleep at night and hunt for food during the day. Some small animals eat and sleep all through the day and night.

Animal families

Most animals are either male or female. It takes a male and a female of the same kind of animal to produce young. Some animals build homes in which to live. Some animals wander from place to place looking for food. Some animals live alone. Some animals live in groups.

These Japanese snow monkeys make their own heat. They are called warm-blooded animals. Mammals and birds are warm-blooded.

This lizard needs to warm itself in the sun. It is called a cold-blooded animal. Reptiles, fish, and insects are cold-blooded.

FOOD

Animals that eat plants are called herbivores. Animals that eat meat are called carnivores. Animals that eat insects are called insectivores. Animals that eat plants, meat, and insects are called omnivores.

Ant

see also: Aardvark, Anteater, Insect

An ant is a small insect. It lives with other ants in a group. This group is called a colony. Some colonies have a few ants. Some colonies have millions of ants. Ants live everywhere except the coldest parts of the world.

ANT FACTS

NUMBER OF KINDS	more than 10,000
COLOR	black, brown, or red
LENGTH	from very tiny to 1 inch
STATUS	common
LIFE SPAN	from a few weeks to 20 years
ENEMIES	aardvarks, anteaters, birds, frogs, lizards, spiders, other insects, people

PLANT AND MEAT EATER

Ants eat many kinds of food. They eat leaves and dead animals. Ants chew their food. This squeezes out the sugary juice. Then ants spit out whatever is left over. Ants eat during the day and night.

antennae to smell other ants and to touch, taste, and hear

strong jaws to hold food, fight enemies, and lift things ten times bigger than the ant

hard covering to protect the inside of an ant

sharp claws to walk up walls and to walk upside down on leaves and twigs

a red ant

Ant families

Each colony has three kinds of ants. The queen ant is a female ant. She spends her whole life laying eggs. The worker ants are female ants. They find food and look after the queen ant and the young ants. Male ants die after they mate with the queen. Some colonies of ants build huge nests below the ground.

Thousands of ants worked together for many years to build this huge nest.

Antarctica

see also: Continent

Antarctica is the fifth largest continent. It is not divided into countries.

The land

Antarctica is covered by ice. Ice covers the valleys, plains, and mountains. The sea is frozen around some of the coast.

Climate, plants, and animals

Antarctica is the coldest continent. The temperature is usually below freezing (32° F). In summer, the sun does not go down for months. In winter, the sun does not come up for months.

Only some mosses and lichens grow in Antarctica. Penguins, seals, whales, and small shrimps called krill live in the ocean around Antarctica.

People in Antarctica

Roald Amundsen was the first person to reach the South Pole. He got there on December 14, 1911. He was from Norway. Scientists are the only people who live in Antarctica. They study the rocks, animals, and climate. Scientists from the United States and Australia have a base at the South Pole. The base is underground. This is where they can be warm and safe from winds and storms.

ANTARCTICA FACTS

SIZE	about 5.4 million square miles
HIGHEST POINT	Vinson Massif—16,864 ft.
ICE	90 per cent of the world's fresh water is in Antarctica's ice
SPECIAL FEATURE	the South Pole, the most southern point on Earth

This is where scientists live and work on Signy Island in Antarctica.

Anteater

see also: Aardvark, Mammal

The anteater is a mammal. It lives in forests and open plains of Central and South America. The biggest anteater is the giant anteater.

ANTEATER FACTS

NUMBER OF KINDS	4
COLOR	gray, brown, black and white
LENGTH	about 6 ft. with tail
HEIGHT	about 27 in.
WEIGHT	44–66 lbs.
STATUS	common
LIFE SPAN	25 years
ENEMIES	jaguars

INSECT EATER

An anteater eats at night from many ant and termite nests. It never eats everything in the nest. That way there will be more the next time the anteater eats.

a color that helps it hide in long grass

long hair to keep warm and dry

nose to smell ants and termites that are underground

long, spiky, sticky tongue to catch ants

walks on knuckles

strong claws for protection and to dig up ants and termites

a tree anteater, or tamandua

Anteater families

Male and female anteaters do not live together. Anteaters have one or two babies at a time. The babies live with their mother for two years. Then they are grown up. An anteater does not make its own home. It often sleeps in another animal's burrow.

The mother carries the baby on her back for the baby's first year.

Antelope

see also: Mammal

An antelope is a mammal. It is a relative of the cow. Most antelope live in Africa. Some live in Asia. Some live on open plains or mountains. Others live in marshes, deserts, or forests.

Antelope families

Female antelope and their young often live in large groups called herds. The herd moves around in its search for food. The females go to the males to mate. The females have one baby at a time.

ANTELOPE FACTS	
NUMBER OF KINDS	more than 100
COLOR	usually brown or gray
HEIGHT	from 10 in. to 6 ft.
WEIGHT	15–1,200 lbs.
STATUS	some endangered
LIFE SPAN	2–5 years
ENEMIES	lions, leopards, wild dogs, wolves, coyotes, people

horns made of bone, sometimes used for fighting

big ears to listen for danger

a male bontebok antelope

strong legs to run as fast as 35 miles per hour

hooves like sheep and cattle

PLANT EATER

Antelope eat grass and shrubs during the day. An antelope eats its food twice. First it swallows the grass. Then later it brings the grass back up to chew it.

Topi antelope and their young listen for danger.

Anthony, Susan B.

Susan B. Anthony was a campaigner for women's rights. She wanted women to have the right to vote.

Anthony protests

Anthony was born on February 15, 1820, in Adams, Massachusetts. She was raised a Quaker. Quakers believe in equality. Anthony became a teacher. She campaigned for equal pay for women teachers and equal education for girls. She also fought to end slavery and to ban the sale of liquor.

Susan B. Anthony

KEY DATES

1820.....Susan B. Anthony is born.
1872.....Anthony is arrested for voting.
1906.....Anthony dies.
1920.....Nineteenth Amendment (passed in 1920) gives women the vote.

Anthony and Stanton

Anthony was not allowed to speak at meetings about slavery and liquor because she was a woman. She decided that if women could vote, then they would have a say. In 1872 Anthony voted in Rochester, New York. She was arrested and fined $100. Anthony worked with Elizabeth Cady Stanton in the women's rights movement. Over many years, she gained some rights for women. Women gained the vote fourteen years after Anthony died.

This cartoon shows the suffragettes Elizabeth Cady Stanton and Susan B. Anthony at a meeting.

DID YOU KNOW?

The government put Anthony's image on a dollar coin in 1979. She was the first woman ever to appear on U.S. money.

Ape

see also: Mammal, Monkey

Apes are large mammals. There are several kinds of apes. There are chimpanzees, gorillas, orangutans, and gibbons. Apes live in Africa and Asia. They are found in forests, woodlands, and rain forests.

Ape families

Gorillas and chimpanzees live in groups. The groups are called bands or troops. Orangutans live by themselves except when a mother and her baby live together. Gibbons live in families. The families include a mother, a father, and their children. Apes usually have one baby at a time. Most apes make a nest in a tree for sleeping. They make a new nest each night.

PLANT, INSECT AND MEAT EATER

Apes eat during the day. All apes eat fruit, leaves, insects, and shoots. Some chimpanzees eat monkeys, too.

A young chimp keeps dry by clinging to its mother's back as she gets a drink of water.

APE FACTS

NUMBER OF KINDS	13
COLOR	black or brown. The orangutan is reddish orange.
HEIGHT	up to 6 ft.
WEIGHT	heaviest ape (male gorilla) up to 600 lbs.
STATUS	some endangered
LIFE SPAN	20–50 years
ENEMIES	People often kill adult apes and take the babies to sell as pets. People also destroy the forests where apes live.

a gibbon

long, hooklike thumb for gripping branches

long arms for swinging through trees

throat sac gives gibbons and orangutans a very loud voice

soft fur

no tail

toes that are used like fingers

flexible feet for holding onto branches

Architecture

see also: Art, Castle, Cathedral, Home

Architecture is the art of planning buildings. Buildings should be safe and strong. People should want to live and work in them. Buildings should look good, too. People who plan buildings are called architects.

Pillars and beams once supported the roof of this building.

The three ways of building

Architects use three plans to make a building. One simple plan is to build pillars or walls. Beams are placed on top of the walls. The beams hold up the roof. Another plan is to use arches. Arches hold the building together. A third plan is to use a strong frame. The frame is made of wood or metal. Walls cover the frame. The frame holds the roof.

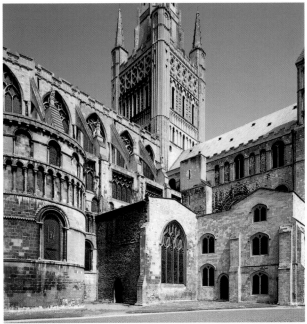

Arches support the walls of this church.

Good buildings

Buildings of today look different from buildings of long ago. But all good buildings are alike in two ways. First, a good building will be right for the job it has to do. A school is different from a house. A house is different from a shopping mall. Second, the building should be made from the right materials. The right materials help the building do its job.

A wooden frame supports the walls and roof of this house.

Arctic

see also: Tundra

The Arctic is the area around the North Pole. It is not a continent. Most of the Arctic is frozen ocean. There is very little land under the ice. However, the Arctic has some islands. Greenland is the biggest island. Parts of North America, Europe, and Asia are inside the Arctic Circle.

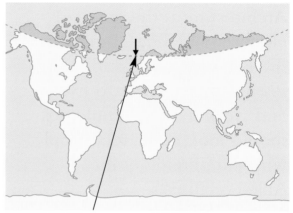

The Arctic Circle is marked with an arrow.

Climate, plants, and animals

The temperature is usually below freezing (32° F). In winter, it is always dark. The sun does not come up. In summer, there is only daylight. The sun never sets. Grasses, flowers, mosses, and lichens grow on the land during the very short summers. Seals and walruses live in the Arctic seas. The biggest animals that live there are polar bears, caribou, and reindeer.

The land inside the Arctic Circle is a treeless plain called a tundra.

People in the Arctic

Some people live in the Arctic. They herd reindeer. They hunt and fish. The first person to go to the North Pole was Robert Peary. He was an American. He reached the North Pole on April 6, 1909.

The United States submarine *Nautilus* sailed under the North Pole in 1958. It sailed in the ocean under the ice.

Argentina

see also: South America

Argentina is the second largest country in South America. It is on the southern tip of South America. It has a long seacoast. The Andes Mountains are in Argentina.

Living in Argentina

The pampas are cool, grassy plains. Farmers raise huge herds of cattle on the pampas. Cowhands are called *gauchos*.

Argentina has many large, modern cities. Thirteen million people live in Buenos Aires. It is the capital city. Spain ruled Argentina until 1810. Many cities and towns have Spanish-style buildings and town squares.

Gauchos ride horses to herd cattle across the grassy pampas.

DID YOU KNOW?

Many of the highest mountains in the Andes Mountains are volcanoes.

Beef is Argentina's national dish. Restaurants serve steaks cooked over open grills.

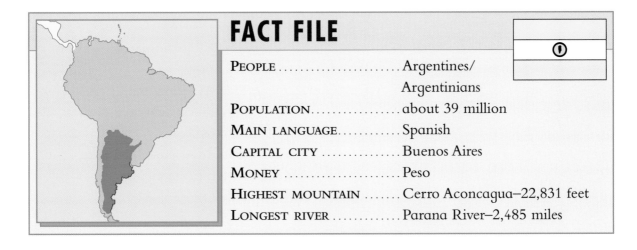

FACT FILE

PEOPLE	Argentines/ Argentinians
POPULATION	about 39 million
MAIN LANGUAGE	Spanish
CAPITAL CITY	Buenos Aires
MONEY	Peso
HIGHEST MOUNTAIN	Cerro Aconcagua–22,831 feet
LONGEST RIVER	Parana River–2,485 miles

Arizona

see also: United States of America

Arizona is a state in the southwestern United States of America. The Southwest is warm and very dry. Parts of Arizona are desert. In other parts, there are high plateaus. One of the most beautiful places in Arizona is the Grand Canyon. It runs through the Colorado Plateau in the northern part of the state.

In the past

Long ago, the Hohokam people lived in Arizona. They built long canals to carry water so they could farm the dry desert land. Later, the Navajo and Apache people came.

Many Native American people from several different tribes still live in Arizona today.

These strange rock formations are found in Monument Valley in northwest Arizona.

DID YOU KNOW?

The Grand Canyon is the world's biggest gorge. It is 277 miles long, up to 15 miles wide, and about 1 mile deep.

Life in Arizona

Manufacturing is the most important industry in Arizona. People there make electronic, transportation, and communications equipment. Mines in Arizona produce over half the copper in the United States. There are cotton farms and many cattle ranches there, too.

Arizona

FACT FILE

BECAME A STATE...	1912 (48th state)
LAND AREA.........	113,635 square miles
	(6th largest land area)
POPULATION	5,580,811
	(18th most populated state)
OTHER NAME	Grand Canyon State
CAPITAL CITY	Phoenix

Arkansas

see also: United States of America

Arkansas is a state in the southern United States of America. In the west and north, the state is mountainous. In the south and east, it is flat. Forests grow in the north in a region named the Ozarks. In the west is Hot Springs National Park, where warm water bubbles out of the ground. The weather is warm in Arkansas, and there is plenty of rain.

Life in Arkansas

Most people in Arkansas live in cities. The biggest city in Arkansas is Little Rock, the state capital. People believe Little Rock got its name from explorer Bernard de la Harpe in 1722. He named it for a rock formation that still stands in the city today.

This is the view from the mountains of Petit Jean State Park.

DID YOU KNOW?

The only diamond mine in the United States is at Crater of Diamond State Park in Murfreesboro, Arkansas. It is represented on Arkansas's state flag by the diamond shape in the center.

Arkansas is a major producer of food and wood products, including paper. Arkansas produces more rice and more poultry than any other state. Farmers in the state also grow cotton and soybeans and raise cattle.

Arkansas

FACT FILE

BECAME A STATE	1836 (25th state)
LAND AREA	52,068 square miles (27th largest land area)
POPULATION	2,725,714 (32nd largest population)
OTHER NAMES	Natural State, Razorback State
CAPITAL CITY	Little Rock

Armstrong, Neil

see also: Moon, Space Exploration

Neil Armstrong was an astronaut. He was the first person to walk on the moon.

Working for NASA
Armstrong was born on August 5, 1930, in Ohio. When he was young, he made model airplanes.

In 1951, Armstrong flew fighter planes in the Korean War. Then he became a test pilot for the National Aeronautics and Space Administration (NASA). NASA was working on rockets that would fly into space. In 1962, Armstrong was chosen to be an astronaut. He first went into space on *Gemini 8* in 1966.

Neil Armstrong

KEY DATES

1930 ..... Neil Armstrong is born.
1962 ..... Armstrong becomes an astronaut.
1966 ..... Armstrong goes on *Gemini 8* mission.
1969 ..... Armstrong lands on the moon.

To the moon and home again
In 1969, Armstrong was chosen to command the *Apollo 11* mission. *Apollo 11* would try to land on the moon. On July 16, 1969, *Apollo 11* lifted off from Florida. Its lunar module landed on the moon on July 20. Armstrong and crew member Buzz Aldrin walked on the moon. They returned safely to Earth.

In 1971, Armstrong left NASA and became a teacher. Later he advised businesses and the government about things to do with space.

When Armstrong stepped on the moon, he said, "That's one small step for man, one giant leap for mankind."

Art

see also: Architecture, Painting, Sculpture

Art is painting and drawing. Art is also architecture and sculpture. All art uses color, lines, textures, patterns, and shapes.

Art can show real people, animals, or things. This is called representational art. Art can also show ideas or feelings. Art does not have to be a picture of something real. This is called abstract art. Some art is both kinds. People go to art galleries or to museums to look at works of art.

How art developed

People have always made art. Very early people made cave paintings. They used natural materials. Since then, people have used many kinds of materials. People have also developed many styles of art.

Vincent Van Gogh (1853–1890)

Vincent Van Gogh was a famous artist. He was born in the Netherlands. He did most of his painting in France. Van Gogh used bright colors. He painted with strong brush strokes. He painted many pictures of nature. His paintings are signed with just his first name, Vincent. Van Gogh's paintings are still very popular.

Van Gogh painted many sunflower paintings. This one is in a museum in London, England.

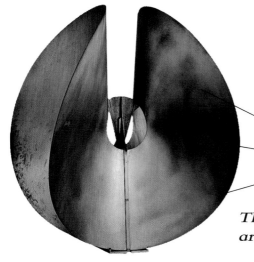

smooth texture

curved lines

warm, bronze color

This sculpture was made by the artist Naum Gabo in 1960.

Asia

see also: Continent

Asia is the biggest of the seven continents. Europe is west of Asia. The Pacific Ocean is to the east. The islands of Japan and Indonesia are part of Asia.

The land

There are large flat, grassy plains in Asia. The world's highest mountain range, the Himalayas, are in Asia. Two of the world's most important rivers, the Ganges and the Huang He, flow through Asia.

Climate, plants, and animals

Northern Asia has freezing temperatures in the winter. It has cool summers. Pine forests grow where it is cold. Brown bears and wolves live in the forests.

The south and east have a hot, wet season and a warm, dry season. Monkeys, snakes, and tigers live in Asia's rain forests.

People in Asia

One-third of all the people in the world live in Asia. Most of the people are farmers. They grow rice, wheat, tea, and cotton. There are also many big cities with factories, businesses, and shops.

ASIA FACTS

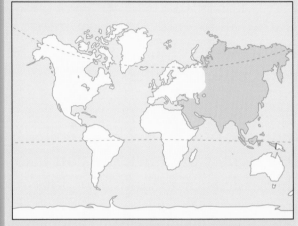

SIZE	17 million square miles
HIGHEST MOUNTAIN	Mount Everest–29,028 ft.
LONGEST RIVER	Yangtze–3,915 miles
SPECIAL FEATURE	Lake Baikal, world's deepest lake–5,315 ft. deep

This is Hong Kong, China. It is a main business center in Asia.

Australia

see also: Aborigines, Australia and Oceania, Marsupial

Australia is a large country. It is an island southeast of Asia. There are mountains in the east. There are hot, dry deserts in the center and the west. There are hot, wet forests in the north.

Living in Australia

The first people in Australia were Aborigines. Early settlers came from Europe. Many people from Asia also came to live in Australia. Australia is a mix of many people.

More than half of the people live in cities. Factory workers make food and machinery. Millions of sheep and cattle graze on farms. The farms are called stations. One-third of all the wool in the world comes from Australia's sheep.

This is the city of Sydney. The very modern-looking Sydney Opera House is built in the harbor.

DID YOU KNOW?

Some children live on remote sheep or cattle stations. They do not go to school. Instead they listen to the School of the Air. It is a kind of two-way radio school.

FACT FILE

Australia and Oceania

PEOPLE	Australians
POPULATION	about 19 million
MAIN LANGUAGES	English, Aboriginal languages
CAPITAL CITY	Canberra
BIGGEST CITY	Sydney
MONEY	Australian dollar
HIGHEST MOUNTAIN	Mount Kosciusko—7,310 ft.
LONGEST RIVER	Darling River—1,702 miles

Australia and Oceania

see also: Aborigines, Australia, Continent, Marsupial

Australia and Oceania is a continent. It is south of Asia. It includes Australia, Tasmania, Papua New Guinea, and New Zealand. It also includes ten thousand small islands.

The land

Australia is the main land. Most of its land is low and flat. Its mountains are the Great Dividing Range.

Australia and Oceania have many islands. Some are made of coral. Some are extinct or active volcanoes. Most of the islands are so small that they do not have names.

Climate, plants, and animals

The center of Australia is desert. Northern Australia is hot. Parts of New Zealand and Papua New Guinea are hot. Sometimes these hot places are very wet. Kangaroos, koalas, crocodiles, and dingoes live in Australia. The flightless kiwi bird lives in New Zealand.

People and countries

Some people in Australia and New Zealand are farmers. They raise cattle and sheep. Most people in Australia and New Zealand live in towns and cities. Most island people live on farms or in fishing villages.

LAND FACTS

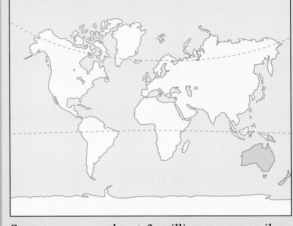

SIZE	about 3 million square miles
HIGHEST MOUNTAIN	Mount Wilhelm in Papua New Guinea–14,793 ft.
LONGEST RIVER	Darling River in Australia–1,702 miles
SPECIAL FEATURE	Uluru, also called Ayers Rock, is a large rock on a plain in Australia

This is a beach on the Solomon Islands in the South Pacific Ocean.

Austria

see also: Europe

Austria is a country in central Europe. It has many mountain ranges. There are wide valleys between them. The country in the east is flat. Winters are cold. Summers are warm.

Living in Austria

Most people live in small towns and villages. Homes in the mountains have overhanging roofs. This keeps the snow away from the house.

Austria is famous for its special cakes and pastries. Every town and village has its own recipes. Austria is also famous for its music. A music festival is held every year in the city of Vienna.

These farm buildings are near the town of Innsbruck.

DID YOU KNOW?

The oldest school in Austria is in Vienna. Benedictine monks opened the school 750 years ago.

Wolfgang Amadeus Mozart (1756–1791)

Mozart was a famous Austrian music composer. He was writing music when he was five years old. He wrote more than 600 pieces of music. He was 35 years old when he died.

FACT FILE

PEOPLE	Austrians
POPULATION	about 8 million
MAIN LANGUAGE	German
CAPITAL CITY	Vienna
MONEY	Euro
HIGHEST MOUNTAIN	Grossglockner–12,457 ft.
LONGEST RIVER	Danube River–1,770 miles

Aztecs

see also: Maya, Mexico

The Aztecs were a group of Native American people. They ruled a part of Mexico about 600 years ago. They conquered their neighbors. They took more and more land. Finally they had a large empire.

What were the Aztecs like?

The Aztecs had a king. He had priests, warriors, and traders to run the country for him. There were also farmers who grew crops and sold the crops at the market.

The Aztecs believed in many gods. They believed that gods controlled the world. The Aztecs prayed to the gods and gave them presents. Sometimes the Aztecs made human sacrifices to the gods.

The great Aztec city Tenochtitlan may have looked like this. It was built in the middle of Lake Texcoco.

KEY DATES

1300 ..... The first Aztecs settle next to Lake Texcoco.
1325 ..... Tenochtitlan, a city in the middle of a lake, is built.
1426–
1515 ..... The Aztec empire grows.
1518 ..... The Spanish reach Mexico.
1519 ..... The Spanish capture Tenochtitlan.
1520 ..... The Aztec empire falls apart.

For what are the Aztecs known?

The Aztecs made beautiful gold jewelry and feather clothes. They wrote with picture writing.

What happened to the Aztecs?

The Spanish conquered the Aztecs in 1519. The Spanish were led by Hernando Cortez. The Aztec empire fell. Some Mexican people today are descendants of the Aztecs.

Bacteria

see also: Virus

Bacteria are some of the smallest living things. Bacteria have one cell. The cell splits into two cells to make more bacteria. There can be many bacteria in a very short time.

How bacteria live
Bacteria live everywhere that they find food. They live in air, soil, and water.

What do bacteria do?
Some bacteria make people and animals ill. Some bacteria are used to make cheese, yogurt, and medicine. Other bacteria are used to make fertilizer, leather, and detergents.

BACTERIA FACTS

SIZE	1 million bacteria could fit on the head of a pin
LIFE SPAN	up to 20 or more years
ENEMIES	antiseptics, antibiotics, white blood cells

thick wall to cover and protect the cell

soft jelly to help it eat food and build up cell parts

thin hairs that help some bacteria swim through liquids

a hipylori bacterium

The picture shows a single bacterium 10,400 times bigger than it really is. This bacteria can cause stomach ulcers.

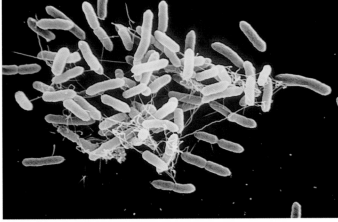

This is a photograph of E. coli *bacteria. It was taken through a microscope. The bacteria look 2,500 times bigger than they really are. A person who studies bacteria is called a bacteriologist.*

PLANT AND MEAT EATER
Bacteria eat all kinds of food. Some bacteria help to break up dead plants, animals, and other waste material.

Badger

see also: Mammal

The badger is a mammal. Badgers live everywhere in Europe. They also live in much of Asia. One kind of badger lives in North America.

PLANT, INSECT, AND MEAT EATER

Badgers eat fruit, roots, eggs, birds, frogs, snails, insects, earthworms, and small rodents. Badgers come out only at night.

BADGER FACTS

NUMBER OF KINDS	8
COLOR	silvery gray, black and white
LENGTH	up to 3 ft.
HEIGHT	about 12 in.
WEIGHT	up to 35 lbs.
STATUS	common
LIFE SPAN	15 years
ENEMIES	People hunt badgers for their hair to make brushes. Many badgers are hit by cars.

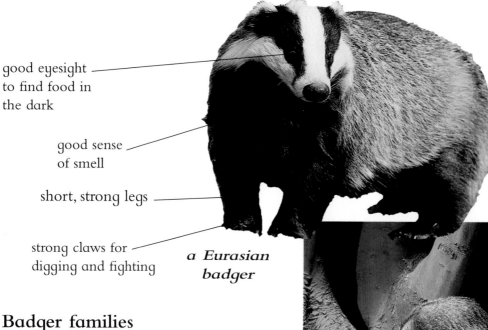

good eyesight to find food in the dark

good sense of smell

short, strong legs

strong claws for digging and fighting

a Eurasian badger

a scent gland that gives it a strong odor

short, stiff hair for protection from thorns

Badger families

The male is called a boar. The female is called a sow. Females have as many as seven babies at a time. The babies are called cubs. They are born in the spring. Badgers live in large families. The family is called a group. American badgers dig burrows in the sides of hills. Eurasian badgers live in forests.

These three young badgers are out at night hunting for earthworms.

Bahamas

see also: Island, North America

The Bahamas is a country in the Atlantic Ocean. It has more than 700 islands. The islands are small and flat. There are 2,000 rocky, mini-islands. There are shallow seas around the islands. Many islands have white, sandy beaches. It is warm all year.

Living in the Bahamas

Most of the people live on one small island. It is called New Providence. Some people work with the tourists who visit the Bahamas. Others fish for a living. Tons of fish are caught. Everyone eats different fish dishes.

The Bahamas has a special festival called *Junkanoo.* It is on the day after Christmas or on New Year's Day. There is music and parades. People wear masks and costumes.

Fishermen sell the fish they catch from their boats. These fishermen are at Potters Cay, Nassau, on New Providence Island.

DID YOU KNOW?

Pirates once hid in the Bahamas. Blackbeard was a famous pirate. He lived on an island in the Bahamas.

North America

FACT FILE

PEOPLE	Bahamians
POPULATION	299 thousand
MAIN LANGUAGES	English, Creole
CAPITAL CITY	Nassau
MONEY	Bahamian dollar
HIGHEST MOUNTAIN	Mount Alvernia—676 ft.

Bald Eagle

see also: Eagle

The bald eagle is a bird. It is the national bird of the United States of America. It is a symbol of the nation.

About bald eagles
The bald eagle is the only eagle that lives just in North America. Bald eagles live near water. They eat fish and small land animals, such as snakes and rabbits. Bald eagles have huge, powerful wings. They can fly very fast and very high.

A symbol of freedom
In 1782, the bald eagle was chosen to represent the nation's strength and freedom. Its picture is used on quarters and dollar bills. It is on official uniforms. It is used on the presidential seal, which is the president's official stamp.

This is how the bald eagle appears on the Great Seal of the United States government.

The Great Seal
The bald eagle forms the center of the Great Seal, the official stamp of the U.S. government. Important government documents carry the Great Seal to show they are real. The bald eagle on the Great Seal holds an olive branch in one claw to symbolize peace. It holds arrows in its other claw to show that Americans are ready to fight for their country. The shield in front of the bald eagle shows that the United States can protect itself.

A bald eagle has a hooked beak for tearing meat.

DID YOU KNOW?

The bald eagle is not really bald. It has white feathers on its head. Long ago, "bald" used to mean white or marked with white. That is why the bald eagle has its name.

Ballet

see also: Dance

Ballet is a way of dancing. It began in Europe in the 1600s. Men and women who dance in a ballet are ballet dancers. Most ballets tell a story. A ballet usually has costumes, scenery, and music.

How a ballet is created

The person who creates the ballet is a choreographer. He or she plans the dance steps. He or she decides how the dancers will show the story. The choreographer works with the dancers and with the people who make the costumes and the scenery.

Sometimes a ballet is danced to music that is already written. Sometimes music is written just for that dance.

How to be a dancer

Training to be a ballet dancer is very hard work. A dancer begins at a young age. Many children go to ballet classes for fun.

This is the ballet Swan Lake. *The music was written by the Russian composer Peter Ilich Tchaikovsky.*

DID YOU KNOW?

All ballet movement is based on five standing positions. All special steps in ballet begin with one of these five positions.

position 1   position 2   position 3   position 4   position 5

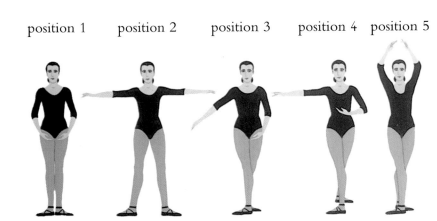

These are the basic standing positions in ballet.

Balloon

see also: Airplane, Transportation

A balloon is a big bag. It is filled with hot air or helium gas. The hot air or gas makes the balloon rise. Balloons were the first flying machines. They were invented more than one hundred years before airplanes.

The first balloons

The Montgolfier brothers of France made the first successful balloon. The first balloons floated with the wind. Later balloons, called airships, were shaped like giant cigars. Airships had engines. They could be steered. They carried passengers. Airships were filled with hydrogen gas. This gas can explode. There were many airship accidents.

The first balloon lifted off in Paris, France. It was bright blue with gold designs.

Today's balloons look like the first balloons, but they are made from light, strong materials.

How we use balloons

Scientists use balloons to carry instruments that check the weather. Some people fly in balloons for fun. Balloons are slow and hard to steer. They are not very useful for carrying people or goods.

People ride in the basket under the balloon.

BALLOON FACTS

INVENTED	1783
BIGGEST	1939, an airship called Graf Zepplin II

Bangladesh

see also: Asia

Bangladesh is a country in Asia. It has many rivers. It has hills in the southeast. The temperature is always very warm. Rain falls in the wet and windy monsoon season. The rain causes floods. The floods make the soil fertile for farming.

DID YOU KNOW?

People in Bangladesh travel on rivers more than they travel on roads. The rivers are also used to carry goods. Rivers are better for travel than roads during the rainy monsoon season.

Living in Bangladesh

Most people live in the country. Many houses are built on platforms. Platforms keep the houses out of the floods. Many people work on farms. Many people catch fish. The plant called jute grows in Bangladesh. People use jute to make bags, rope, and mats. Bangladesh is known for its fish curry. Mustard oil is used to flavor food.

Stilts keep the houses out of the flood waters.

Asia

FACT FILE

PEOPLE	Bangladeshi
POPULATION	about 141 million
MAIN LANGUAGES	Bengali, English
CAPITAL CITY	Dhaka
MONEY	Taka
HIGHEST MOUNTAIN	Mount Keokradong—4,034 ft.
LONGEST RIVER	Ganges River—1,558 miles

Bar Code

see also: Computer, Laser

A bar code is a label. It is a pattern made of black and white lines. The lines are in a square or rectangular shape. Most things that are sold have a bar code.

How bar codes work

Supermarkets use bar codes. The cashier moves each item across a scanner. A laser light in the scanner bounces off only the white lines of the bar code. The scanner "reads" the bar code. A computer understands the pattern that the scanner read. The pattern is a code. The computer prints a list of what was bought and how much each item costs.

Other uses for bar codes

Shops and factories use bar codes to count the items they sell or use. This tells them when to reorder supplies. When a shelf looks empty, a bar code scanner reads the bar code on the shelf. The code is given to a computer. The computer prints an order to refill the shelf.

Libraries put bar codes on each book. The bar code is read by a scanner when the book is checked out. The computer keeps track of the books that are out on loan.

The store clerk is using a bar code scanner. He is checking the price on a carton of orange juice.

ISBN 0-435-02443-4

9 780435 024437

This is a bar code for a book. It is used when a book is sold in a bookstore. It is used to keep track of the books stored in a warehouse.

Barbados

see also: Hurricane, North America

Barbados is a small island country. It is in the Atlantic Ocean. It is north of South America. Coral reefs surround the island. The weather is always very warm. Barbados has a dry season from December to May. The rest of the year is wet.

Living in Barbados

Most people live on the coast. The people work with tourists. The tourists come to enjoy the sandy beaches and warm seas. Some of the people are farmers. They grow sugar cane.

A festival called Cropover is held every summer. Cropover celebrates freedom. There is calypso music, dancing, and parades. The people make and eat special foods. They cook fish with spices and pepper.

Sugar cane is cut and stacked by hand. It goes to factories where it is made into products.

DID YOU KNOW?

Barbados is in the hurricane zone. Storm winds can knock down buildings and trees. Winds can reach speeds of 155 mph.

North America

FACT FILE

PEOPLE	Barbadians
POPULATION	278 thousand
MAIN LANGUAGES	English, Creole
CAPITAL CITY	Bridgetown
MONEY	Barbados dollar
HIGHEST MOUNTAIN	Mount Hillaby–1,115 ft.

Barge

see also: River, Transportation, Waterway

A barge is a boat that floats in shallow water. It usually has a flat bottom. Most barges have no mast or sail. They are towed or pushed by another boat.

A horse tows this barge in England in the early 1800s.

The first barges

Barges were first used to move large and heavy things on water. This was easier than moving things over land. Horses or mules pulled the first barges. The barges carried coal and wood on canals. Canals are waterways dug through land. Later, engines did the work of pulling. Today some barges are towed or pushed by powerful boats called tugboats.

How we use barges

Barges are still used to carry heavy loads on the world's big rivers. Sometimes two or three barges are towed together like cars on a train.

A tugboat is pushing these barges on the Mississippi River. Barges are used on rivers and waterways.

DID YOU KNOW?

Sometimes people make barges into floating houses. They live on the barges or take a floating vacation.